DON'T BELIEVE THE LIES

A 30-DAY JOURNEY TO BREAK FREE AND LIVE IN GOD'S TRUTH

DR. AYO MOSES

DON'T BELIEVE THE LIES

Copyright © 2025 Dr. Ayo Moses
ISBN: 978-1-965593-61-5

ISBN: 978-1-965593-61-5 All rights reserved. No part of this publication may be reproduced, distributed, or transmitted in any form or by any means, including photocopying, recording, or other electronic or mechanical methods without the prior written permission of the author except in the case of brief quotations embodied in reviews and certain other non-commercial uses permitted by copyright law.

Published by Cornerstone Publishing

A Division of Cornerstone Creativity Group LLC
Info@thecornerstonepublishers.com
www.thecornerstonepublishers.com

Author's Contact

Email: info@ayomosesmd.com
Website: www.ayomosesmd.com
Instagram: @ayomosesmd

To invite Dr. Moses for church services, Christian conferences, or faith-based leadership events, kindly visit **www.ayomosesmd.com**

Printed in the United States of America.

DON'T BELIEVE THE LIES

DEDICATION

To God, the Author of truth and the Giver of life. I thank You for Your grace, wisdom, and strength that made this work possible. I pray that every page draws readers closer to You.

To my wife, Lola, whose love, wisdom, strength, and unwavering support remind me daily of God's faithfulness.

To my children, Ariyo and Ayoka, who inspire me to leave a legacy of faith and truth.

To my spiritual parents, who daily model perseverance, prayer, and purpose, and continue to lay the blueprint that paves the path to my future.

To my biological parents, whose sacrifices, prayers, and example shaped the foundation of my life.

To my sisters and the Anointed Pacesetters family, whose love, encouragement, and resilience remind me of the gift of family.

To the Cornerstone Publishing team, whose excellence and creativity helped bring this vision to life.

And to every believer who has wrestled with lies yet dares to embrace the truth: This book is for you.

CONTENTS

Introduction vii

Lie 1: You're Not Enough 1
Lie 2: If They Really Knew You, They Wouldn't Love You 4
Lie 3: You'll Never Change 7
Lie 4: You're Too Broken To Be Used By God 10
Lie 5: You Are Your Past 13
Lie 6: You're Always The Second Choice 16
Lie 7: You Have To Perform To Be Accepted 19
Lie 8: You're Not Gifted Enough 22
Lie 9: Nobody Cares About You 25
Lie 10: You're A Burden 28
Lie 11: You Missed Your Calling 31
Lie 12: God Can't Use Someone Like You 34
Lie 13: You Should Be Further By Now 37
Lie 14: Your Life Has No Impact 40
Lie 15: You'll Never Find Your Purpose 43
Lie 16: You'll Always End Up Alone 46
Lie 17: You Don't Deserve Real Love 49

Lie 18: People Always Leave 52

Lie 19: If You Set Boundaries, They'll Stop
Loving You... 55

Lie 20: You Have To Settle To Be Loved.................. 58

Lie 21: God Is Disappointed In You 61

Lie 22: God's Not Listening 63

Lie 23: God's Promises Aren't For You..................... 65

Lie 24: God Doesn't Care About The Small Stuff .. 68

Lie 25: You've Gone Too Far For God To Still
Love You 71

Lie 26: It's Too Late To Start Over 74

Lie 27: Things Will Never Get Better........................ 76

Lie 28: This Struggle Is Forever 79

Lie 29: Your Best Days Are Behind You................... 82

Lie 30: You'll Always Be Stuck................................... 85

Conclusion: After 30 Days, What Next? 88

INTRODUCTION

Every day, we are bombarded with lies, not always shouted, but whispered.

"You're not enough."

"You'll never change."

"God has forgotten you."

They show up in quiet moments, in sleepless nights, in our scrolls, in our silence. Left unchecked, these mind games shape how we see ourselves, how we treat others, and how we relate to God. But here's the truth:

Freedom begins in the mind, and it's fueled by truth.

On this journey of becoming, I've witnessed how lies can quietly damage the spirit, drain the body, strain relationships, and affect so many areas of our lives. But I've also seen the power of God's truth to bring healing, clarity, and confidence.

Jesus said it best: **"You will know the truth, and the truth will set you free"** (John 8:32) NLT. This freedom isn't reserved for the perfect. It's not delayed until the storm passes. It starts when you begin to think differently, when you align your beliefs with God's Word and not your wounds.

This 30-day devotional was written to walk with you. It is designed to help you expose and evict the lies the enemy has tried to plant, and to replace them with the unshakable promises of God. Each day includes:

- One lie the enemy wants you to believe
- A reflection rooted in biblical truth
- A prayer to center your heart
- An affirmation to renew your mind

Whether you're healing from heartbreak, wrestling with identity, or simply tired of being stuck, this journey is for you.

You were never meant to live under the weight of shame, fear, or falsehood. You were created to walk in **truth, purpose, and freedom.**

So let's begin. Not just another devotional, but a declaration: **You don't have to believe the lies anymore!**

Lie #1

YOU'RE NOT ENOUGH

Truth: *"I praise you because I am fearfully and wonderfully made; your works are wonderful, I know that full well."* (Psalm 139:14) **NIV**

REFLECTION:

The lie of "not enough" sneaks in through the back door of comparison.

It shows up when a student glances at someone else's grades and silently wonders if she'll ever measure up. It whispers to the young man watching others climb the career ladder faster, making him question his value. Over time, that lie doesn't just bruise your confidence, it convinces you that something is missing in you by design.

But let's set the record straight: God never made a mistake when He made you.

Who would've guessed that an orphan girl named Esther, hidden in obscurity, would one day become the very key to saving a nation? She wasn't the obvious pick, but she was God's choice. Or Jeremiah, a hesitant young man who felt underqualified and overwhelmed, yet was handpicked by God to speak truth to nations. In both stories, God's pattern is clear: **He doesn't choose the most prepared, He prepares the ones He's chosen.**

When the enemy whispers, *"You're not enough,"* the cross answers, *"Christ in you is more than enough."*

You're not called to compete, you're called to **complete** what He's assigned to you. And what the world calls a weakness? God calls a setup for His strength to shine. You are enough!

PRAYER:

Lord, reveal the lie of inadequacy that infiltrates my heart and mind. Remind me daily that my worth is found in Your design, not in human comparison. Teach me to rest in the truth that I am fearfully and wonderfully made. Amen.

AFFIRMATION:

I am enough in Christ. I lack nothing. I am who God says I am fearfully and wonderfully made.

_____

_____

_____

_____

_____

_____

_____

_____

_____

_____

_____

Lie #2

IF THEY REALLY KNEW YOU, THEY WOULDN'T LOVE YOU

Truth: *"Nothing in all creation will ever be able to separate us from the love of God."* (Romans 8:39) **NLT**

REFLECTION:

This lie thrives in the silence of shame, where secrets fester and self-worth begins to rot.

It whispers that if people ever saw *the real you*: the broken chapters, the hidden battles, the past you're trying to outgrow, they'd walk away. So, you hide. You curate. You smile while silently struggling. You succeed professionally but secretly carry regret. And all the while, the fear lingers: *What if I'm only loved because they don't know the whole story?*

But here's the truth: **God knows every detail, and He never looked away.**

When Jesus called out Zacchaeus from the crowd, He wasn't inviting a polished saint. He was calling a man the world had labeled a fraud and a failure. And yet, Jesus went to his house, broke bread with him, and changed his future. Mary Magdalene? Her story was laced with pain and rejection, yet Jesus chose her to be the first witness of His resurrection. Why? Because **God's love shines brightest in full view of your story.**

You don't have to filter your pain for God to find you lovable. He already sees it all and still chooses you. And the people He sends into your life? They won't need the edited version. They'll love the healed and healthy you.

The lie says: "If they knew, they'd leave."

The truth says: "You are fully known and still fully loved."

PRAYER:

Father, break the power of shame that urges me to conceal myself. Thank You for loving me openly, with nothing hidden. Teach me to find security in Your love and trust that You place people in my life who will love me genuinely. Amen.

AFFIRMATION:

I am fully known and fully loved. I do not have to hide to be accepted, God sees me and still chooses me.

_____

_____

_____

_____

_____

_____

Lie #3

YOU'LL NEVER CHANGE

Truth: *"Anyone who belongs to Christ has become a new person. The old life is gone; a new life has begun!"* (2 Corinthians 5:17) **NLT**

REFLECTION:

Few lies feel heavier than the belief that you're stuck for good.

This lie often surfaces after repeated failures. The person who keeps falling back into addiction. The one who promises not to lash out again but ends up shouting anyway. The cycle of shame grows tighter, and eventually, the enemy's voice gets louder: *This is just who you are. Change is impossible.*

But God never defines you by your worst moment. He defines you by your **new identity** in Christ.

Just look at Jacob. Known for deception and manipulation, he lived with a reputation that matched his name. But one night, everything changed. He wrestled with God, and though he came out limping, he also came out renamed. Jacob became Israel, no longer a schemer, but a father of nations. That transformation didn't erase his past, but it redefined his future.

God still rewrites stories like that today. He specializes in turning breakdowns into breakthroughs and messes into messages. The change you long for may not happen overnight, but it is already unfolding. His Spirit works in layers, not lightning bolts.

PRAYER:

Lord, silence the voice that claims I cannot change. Remind me daily that Your power transforms lives. Help me release old labels and embrace the new identity You've given me in Christ. Amen.

AFFIRMATION:

I am a new creation. Change is not only possible, it is already happening in me through Christ.

Lie #4

YOU'RE TOO BROKEN TO BE USED BY GOD

Truth: *"My grace is all you need. My power works best in weakness."* (2 Corinthians 12:9) **NLT**

REFLECTION:

Brokenness has a way of making you feel benched.

The enemy will point to your past like it's a permanent record. Divorce. Addiction. Failure. Regret. He'll convince you that your scars are a liability and that ministry, influence, or calling is only for the flawless. But here's what the enemy forgets to mention: **God does His best work with broken pieces.**

Naomi walked back into Bethlehem with nothing but grief. Her heart was heavy, her hope was gone, and her hands were empty. She called herself "bitter" and believed her story was over. But God was just getting started. Through Ruth, her equally broken daughter-in-law, Naomi's life became part of the redemptive lineage of Jesus. Her brokenness didn't cancel her purpose. It made room for God's grace to shine even brighter.

Look through Scripture and you'll find the same pattern. Moses was a murderer. David was an adulterer. Paul was a persecutor. Yet each one was handpicked to carry out some of the greatest assignments in history. Why? Because **God doesn't need perfection to display His power. He just needs surrender.**

PRAYER:

Lord, thank You for reminding me that weakness does not hinder Your work; it opens the door for Your power. Use my scars as testimonies of Your grace, and may my brokenness bring You glory. Amen.

AFFIRMATION:

God's power is made perfect in my weakness. My story, with all its flaws, brings Him glory.

_____

_____

_____

_____

_____

_____

_____

_____

_____

_____

Lie #5

YOU ARE YOUR PAST

Truth: *"I have swept away your sins like a cloud. I have scattered your offenses like the morning mist."*
(Isaiah 44:22) **NLT**

REFLECTION:

The past can follow you like an unwanted shadow, trying to convince you it still has the final word.

Maybe you made a mistake that still haunts you. Maybe you grew up in dysfunction and wonder if you'll ever rise above it. Or maybe you hurt someone years ago, and even after asking for forgiveness, the guilt still lingers. That's where the enemy loves to operate in the echo chamber of shame. He whispers, *"This is who you really are. You'll never escape your past."*

But God has a different word for you: **forgiven**.

Isaiah describes it beautifully: your sins, once heavy and looming, are swept away like a morning mist. That means what felt permanent is not. God's mercy is not symbolic. It's surgical. It cuts through shame and removes the stain completely.

Look at King Manasseh. His résumé was filled with idolatry, bloodshed, and rebellion. By all accounts, his story should have ended in disgrace. But when he turned to God in repentance, God listened. Not only did He forgive Manasseh, He restored him. His past didn't disqualify him, it became the backdrop for radical redemption.

You are not the sum of your sins. You are the product of His mercy.

PRAYER:

Lord, thank You for the gift of forgiveness. Help me to let go of my past and embrace the new life You have given me. May I live in the freedom of my identity in Christ. Amen.

AFFIRMATION:

I am not defined by my past. I am redeemed, restored, and renewed by the mercy of God.

Lie #6

YOU'RE ALWAYS THE SECOND CHOICE

Truth: *"You didn't choose me. I chose you."*
(John 15:16) **NLT**

REFLECTION:

Rejection has a way of digging deep. It doesn't just wound, it rewrites how you see yourself.

Maybe you were the child who was always picked last. Or the young adult passed over for a job, a role, or a relationship. Over time, those moments begin to shape a painful identity: *I'm not what people want. I'm never the first choice. I'm just the backup plan.*

But that's not how God sees you.

When Jesus looked at His disciples, ordinary fishermen, tax collectors, men the world would have passed by, He said something radical: *"You didn't choose me. I chose you."* His words weren't accidental. They were affirming. God is not in the business of random selection. He picks on purpose, with purpose.

Consider Leah. Always compared. Always overlooked. Living in the shadow of her sister Rachel. And yet, God chose *her* to carry the lineage that would birth Judah and eventually, Jesus. The one man overlooked became the vessel for a royal bloodline.

Rejection from people doesn't cancel your position in God. If anything, it sets the stage for Him to reveal that **you were never second in His eyes.** *You are God's first choice for the assignment on your life. You're not a backup plan. You're His beloved from the beginning.*

PRAYER:

Father, thank You for reminding me that I am not overlooked but chosen. Heal the wounds of rejection and help me find peace in the assurance that Your choice holds more significance than human approval. Amen.

AFFIRMATION:

I am God's first choice. I am not overlooked; I am handpicked and highly favored.

Lie #7

YOU HAVE TO PERFORM TO BE ACCEPTED

Truth: *"It is by grace you have been saved, through faith… not by works, so that no one can boast."*
(Ephesians 2:8–9) **NIV**

REFLECTION:

We live in a world where approval feels like a paycheck, something you must earn.

As a child, maybe you only felt noticed when you got good grades. As an adult, you might feel seen only when you're producing, exceeding, or outperforming. Even in close relationships, love can feel conditional. Slowly, a toxic belief takes root: *I am only as valuable as what I can do.*

But God's Kingdom doesn't run on performance. It runs on **grace**.

Look at the thief on the cross. He had no résumé. No record of service. No time to prove himself. Yet in a single moment of faith, Jesus welcomed him into eternity. Why? Because acceptance in God's family isn't based on effort. It is based on **faith in Christ's finished work.**

You don't have to hustle for God's love. You don't have to earn His attention. You already have it.

Grace doesn't say, *"Work harder."* Grace says, *"Come as you are."* God didn't wait for you to clean yourself up before loving you. He accepted you before your first success, and He still loves you after every failure. *You don't have to perform to be accepted. You are accepted because of what Jesus already performed for you. God's love is not a reward for good behavior. It's a gift to the surrendered.*

PRAYER:

Lord, free me from the pressure to perform for acceptance. Teach me to rest in Your grace and to live from love, not for love. Remind me daily that I am already secure in Christ. Amen.

AFFIRMATION:

I do not have to earn God's love, I live from it. His grace is sufficient.

Lie #8

YOU'RE NOT GIFTED ENOUGH

Truth: *"We have different gifts, according to the grace given to each of us."* (Romans 12:6) **NIV**

REFLECTION:

Comparison is a silent thief. It doesn't just steal joy, it robs you of confidence in what God has placed inside you.

You see someone sing with power, and suddenly your voice feels small. You watch a preacher captivate a crowd, and you begin to question your own calling. You scroll through highlight reels and wonder why your life feels so ordinary. The whisper begins: *You're not gifted enough. Maybe God skipped you.*

But that is a lie.

Scripture reminds us that **God is the one who gives gifts**, and He does so with precision and purpose. Your gift wasn't an afterthought. It was handcrafted, wrapped in grace, and wired for impact. It's not supposed to look like someone else's; it's meant to reach people that only *you* can reach.

Throughout Scripture, God uses uniquely gifted people to fulfill His plans. Bezalel was an artist chosen to design the beauty of the Tabernacle. Deborah led with wisdom and courage. Timothy, though soft-spoken, pastored churches with faithfulness and strength. Their gifts didn't look alike, but every one of them mattered.

You don't have to be louder to be valuable. You don't have to imitate others to be impactful. **You just have to use what God gave you.** *Your gift is enough, because God gave it, and it has purpose. Your gifts, however hidden, were handpicked for impact.*

PRAYER:

Father, thank You for the grace of unique gifts. Silence the voice of comparison and help me see the value in what You've placed in me. Teach me to use my gifts boldly and faithfully for Your glory. Amen.

AFFIRMATION:

I am gifted by God with something the world needs. I will not downplay my calling.

_____

_____

_____

_____

_____

_____

_____

_____

_____

_____

_____

_____

Lie #9

NOBODY CARES ABOUT YOU

Truth: *"Give all your worries and cares to God, for he cares about you."* (1 Peter 5:7) **NLT**

REFLECTION:

Loneliness doesn't always shout. Sometimes, it just quietly settles in.

It shows up when you move to a new place and feel invisible in the crowd. When your phone stays silent, or when you scroll through other people's happy moments and wonder if anyone would notice if you disappeared. That's when the lie creeps in: *Nobody sees me. Nobody cares.*

But even in those silent seasons, **God is never absent.**

Hagar knows what that feels like. Abandoned in the wilderness, heartbroken and alone, she cried out in despair. And right there, in the middle of nowhere, God met her. He revealed Himself as **El Roi**, the God who sees. He didn't ignore her pain. He didn't walk past her situation. He stopped, spoke, and stayed.

The same God who saw Hagar sees you. He sees every tear, every moment you've felt unseen, every ache you've tried to hide. And He cares deeply.

The absence of people does not mean the absence of love. God's love is not dependent on likes, texts, or invitations. **It's steady, personal, and constant, even when no one else shows up.** *God sees you, knows you, and cares more than you can imagine. You're not invisible to the One who made you, you're invaluable.*

PRAYER:

Father, thank You for caring for me in both significant and small ways. When loneliness whispers lies, remind me of Your faithful love. Surround me with reminders of Your presence and people who reflect Your care. Amen.

AFFIRMATION:

God cares about me. I am never unseen, never unloved, never forgotten.

_____

_____

_____

_____

_____

_____

_____

_____

_____

_____

_____

Lie #10
YOU'RE A BURDEN

Truth: *"Carry each other's burdens, and in this way you will fulfill the law of Christ."* (Galatians 6:2) **NIV**

REFLECTION:

This lie often starts in silence.

It can take root in childhood, when a sensitive child is told to stop being dramatic. It can grow in adulthood, when someone battling anxiety fears they'll push people away if they open up. Even in the church, it shows up when someone sits quietly during a storm, thinking, *I don't want to be a burden. I don't want to be too much.*

But God has never seen your pain as a problem.

When Elijah collapsed under a broom tree, exhausted and overwhelmed, he told God he wanted to give up. He didn't filter his feelings. He didn't package his pain. And God didn't reject him. Instead, God sent an angel to meet him with food, water, and rest. No rebuke. Just care. Just presence. Just grace.

Your emotions are not too heavy for God. And they are not too heavy for the people He's placed in your life either.

The Kingdom of God is built on **community**, not self-containment. You were never meant to do life alone. You were never meant to carry everything alone. Being honest is not weakness. Asking for help is not failure. Letting others walk with you is not a burden, it's a blessing. *You are worthy of support, and God designed you for community.*

PRAYER:

Lord, thank You for creating me for community. Heal the fear that my struggles make me unworthy of love. Teach me to lean on others with humility and to carry others with compassion, reflecting the love of Christ. Amen.

AFFIRMATION:

I am not a burden, I am a blessing. God has placed people in my life to walk with me, not to judge me.

_____

_____

_____

_____

_____

_____

_____

_____

_____

_____

Lie #11

YOU MISSED YOUR CALLING

Truth: *"The gifts and the calling of God are irrevocable."* (Romans 11:29) **ESV**

REFLECTION:

One of the enemy's favorite tactics is convincing you that your moment has passed.

Maybe you let go of a dream years ago and now wonder if it's too late to pick it back up. Maybe you spent years raising children, caring for family, or just surviving, and now you feel like the window to pursue your calling has closed. You may even whisper to yourself, *If I had made different choices earlier, maybe God could have used me.*

But here's the truth: **God's calling doesn't expire and** *delay doesn't cancel destiny.*

Jonah tried to run from his assignment. He didn't just delay his obedience, he boarded a ship going in the opposite direction. And yet, after all the detours, the mistakes, the storm, and the belly of a fish, Scripture tells us, *"The word of the Lord came to Jonah a second time."* God didn't change His mind. He didn't throw Jonah away. He simply reissued the call.

Your detour did not disqualify you. In fact, it might be the very thing God uses to make your calling even more powerful.

He's not just the Redeemer of people, **He's the Redeemer of time, purpose, and calling.** No season is wasted. No story is too messy. And no dream is too delayed for God to breathe life into it again. *God's calling still stands, and He's not done with you yet. What He started, He's still able to fulfill.*

PRAYER:

Father, thank You that Your calling is never revoked. Where I feel delayed or disqualified, remind me that

You are still at work. Redeem my detours and awaken the gifts You have placed within me for Your glory. Amen.

AFFIRMATION:

God's calling on my life still stands. It's not too late, I'm right on time in His hands.

Lie #12

GOD CAN'T USE SOMEONE LIKE YOU

Truth: *"God chose the lowly things of this world… so that no one may boast before him."*
(1 Corinthians 1:28–29) **NIV**

REFLECTION:

This lie usually grows in the shadows of self-doubt.

You look at your past and feel disqualified. You see your limitations and feel unworthy. Maybe you didn't grow up in church. Maybe you still struggle with habits you thought you'd be free from by now. Maybe you compare yourself to others and think, *God uses people like them, not people like me.*

But that is not the way God works.

Rahab's story is proof. She wasn't known for purity or prestige. She was known for her past. And yet, when the moment came, she made a courageous decision to trust the God of Israel. That one act of faith shifted history. She didn't just survive Jericho's fall, she stepped into a legacy of faith so powerful that her name appears in the lineage of Jesus.

God doesn't require perfection. He looks for **willing hearts and surrendered lives.** Your scars, your struggles, your setbacks, they don't disqualify you. They make your story more powerful.

From Moses who stuttered to Rahab who was labeled, Scripture is filled with people God used **not despite their flaws, but through them.** He doesn't call the perfect. He perfects the called.

You are exactly the kind of person God uses to show off His grace, the exact kind of person God delights in using: unlikely, imperfect, but available. That's all He needs.

PRAYER:

Lord, thank You that You choose what the world rejects. Help me surrender every flaw and failure to You, trusting that You can use all of it for Your glory. Amen.

AFFIRMATION:

God can use all of me: flaws, failures, and faith. I am chosen for impact.

_____

_____

_____

_____

_____

_____

_____

Lie #13

YOU SHOULD BE FURTHER BY NOW

Truth: *"He who began a good work in you will carry it on to completion until the day of Christ Jesus."* (Philippians 1:6) **NIV**

REFLECTION:

This lie often creeps in when you're looking sideways instead of upward.

A friend gets married while you're still single. A peer starts their business while you're just finding your footing. Someone in ministry launches their platform while you're still waiting to be noticed. And before you know it, the enemy begins to whisper: *You're behind. You should be further by now.*

But God is not rushed by human timelines. He is not measuring your life against someone else's highlight reel. **He's forming you on His schedule, not the world's.**

Joseph had dreams of greatness as a teenager. He saw glimpses of leadership and influence. But before the dream came to pass, he was betrayed, enslaved, and forgotten in a prison cell. From the outside, it looked like delay. But in God's eyes, **it was development.** And when the right moment came, Joseph stepped into his purpose, not a second too soon or too late.

Your waiting is not wasted. Your progress is not slow. Your journey is not off-track. **God knows the exact timing for your elevation.** Be patient, *you're in process, and God's timing is always right on time. You're not behind, you're being built.*

PRAYER:

Father, help me release the burden of comparison. Teach me to trust Your timing and view delays not as denials but as preparation. Remind me that the good work You began will surely be completed. Amen.

AFFIRMATION:

I am exactly where God needs me to be. My pace has purpose.

Lie #14

YOUR LIFE HAS NO IMPACT

Truth: *"Let your light shine before others, that they may see your good deeds and glorify your Father in heaven."* (Matthew 5:16) **NIV**

REFLECTION:

This lie usually shows up in the ordinary, in the quiet places where it seems no one is watching.

It whispers to the mom wiping counters and calming tantrums. To the teacher who keeps showing up without applause. To the believer who prays faithfully, encourages quietly, and serves in unseen places. It says, *You're not doing anything important. Your life doesn't matter.*

But the truth is: **Heaven sees what earth overlooks.**

Dorcas was not a prophet or a preacher. She didn't lead armies or pen scriptures. She sewed clothes and served widows. Yet her compassion left such a mark that when she died, her entire community wept. They brought her body to Peter, begging for a miracle. And God answered. Dorcas was raised to life, not because she had a public platform, but because her private acts of love mattered deeply.

The same is true for you.

Every smile. Every prayer. Every note of encouragement. Every unseen act of kindness. **You are planting seeds that will bear fruit in ways you may never fully see.** Your life is not small, it's sacred. And God is using it to light up dark places.

You are making a difference, and your obedience is echoing in eternity.

PRAYER:

Lord, quiet the voice that says my life doesn't matter. Remind me that every act of love, every prayer, and every moment of faithfulness shines brightly in

Your eyes. Help me to live each day with confidence, knowing my impact is for Your glory. Amen.

AFFIRMATION:

My life matters. I am light in a dark world, and I shine for God's glory.

_____

_____

_____

_____

_____

_____

_____

_____

_____

Lie #15

YOU'LL NEVER FIND YOUR PURPOSE

Truth: *"For we are God's handiwork, created in Christ Jesus to do good works, which God prepared in advance for us to do."* (Ephesians 2:10) **NIV**

REFLECTION:

The search for purpose can feel like wandering through fog.

You try different things, take a few risks, face some failures, and wonder if you'll ever figure out why you're here. A young adult unsure of their career path. A parent who paused their dreams for others.

A believer who's served for years but still feels uncertain. The enemy whispers, *You're lost. You missed it. You'll never find your purpose.*

But purpose isn't something you stumble across by accident. **It unfolds as you walk with God.**

Ruth wasn't chasing a platform or a title. She was simply choosing loyalty, integrity, and obedience, staying close to Naomi when it would've been easier to walk away. Yet, through that one decision, God positioned her in a divine storyline that led to the birth of the Messiah.

Purpose often shows up when you're just doing the next right thing.

You don't have to have it all figured out today. You don't need a five-year plan or a perfect track record. What you need is a heart that says, *Yes, Lord*, even when the path isn't clear. As you keep moving forward in faith, **purpose will find you right where obedience placed you.**

PRAYER:

Father, thank You that my life is not aimless. Help me to trust You with the unfolding of my purpose.

Teach me to walk in obedience today, confident that You prepared good works for me long before I began. Amen.

AFFIRMATION:

God has a purpose for me, and I am walking in it, one step at a time.

_____

_____

_____

_____

_____

_____

_____

_____

Lie #16

YOU'LL ALWAYS END UP ALONE

Truth: *"Never will I leave you; never will I forsake you."* (Hebrews 13:5) **NIV**

REFLECTION:

Loneliness doesn't just visit, it lingers. And the enemy knows how to use it.

You can be surrounded by people and still feel invisible. You can laugh in public and still ache in private. The lie begins to echo in those quiet, vulnerable moments: *Everyone leaves. No one stays. You'll always end up alone.*

But God's presence is not seasonal. **It is constant. Unshakable. Personal.**

Joseph had every reason to feel abandoned. His brothers betrayed him. His freedom was taken. His integrity landed him in prison. And yet, over and over, Scripture highlights one powerful phrase: *"The Lord was with Joseph."* Not just on the mountaintop, but in the pit. Not just in the palace, but in the prison.

Alone is never the final word when **Emmanuel**, *God with us*, is your companion.

And here's the deeper truth: God doesn't just offer His presence, He also prepares **divine connections**. Relationships rooted in covenant, not convenience. People who won't just walk with you when it's easy, but stand by you when it's hard.

So don't give up. Don't settle. Don't let loneliness redefine your identity. God is with you and He's preparing connections that last.

PRAYER:

Lord, thank You for Your constant presence. Heal the fear of abandonment that tries to take root in my heart. Teach me to trust that You are with me and that You bring the right relationships into my life at the right time. Amen.

AFFIRMATION:

I am never truly alone. God is with me, and He's preparing divine connections.

_____

_____

_____

_____

_____

_____

_____

_____

_____

_____

_____

Lie #17

YOU DON'T DESERVE REAL LOVE

Truth: *"I have loved you with an everlasting love; I have drawn you with unfailing kindness."*
(Jeremiah 31:3) **NIV**

REFLECTION:

Wounds from the past can leave lasting echoes.

Maybe you were abandoned by someone who promised to stay. Maybe you were raised in a home where love was conditional or withheld. Maybe someone once looked you in the eyes and told you that you were hard to love, and a part of you believed them.

The enemy uses those moments to whisper, *You're not worth it. You don't deserve real love.*

But God tells a different story.

In the book of Hosea, we see one of the most radical expressions of love. Hosea was commanded to love Gomer, a woman who repeatedly walked away. And every time she did, Hosea was called to pursue her again. Not because she earned it, but because God wanted to show what His love looks like, faithful, pursuing, covenant love that keeps reaching even when it's rejected.

This is the kind of love God offers you.

His love doesn't back off when you mess up. It doesn't vanish when you feel unworthy. It isn't based on what you've done, but on who He is. And because His love heals and restores, **He will teach you to recognize and receive love that reflects Him, pure, honest, and whole.**

PRAYER:

Father, thank You for loving me with an everlasting love. Heal the wounds that whisper I am unworthy of it. Teach me to rest in Your unfailing kindness and to recognize love that reflects Your truth. Amen.

AFFIRMATION:

I am deeply loved by God. I deserve love that is healthy, whole, and holy.

_____

_____

_____

_____

_____

_____

_____

_____

_____

_____

_____

Lie #18

PEOPLE ALWAYS LEAVE

Truth: *"Though my father and mother forsake me, the Lord will receive me."* (Psalm 27:10) **NIV**

REFLECTION:

Abandonment doesn't just wound, it reshapes the way we trust.

Maybe it started in childhood, when someone who was supposed to stay walked away. Maybe it happened in a relationship, a friendship, or even within the church. Over time, the fear settles in your heart like a warning sign: *Don't get too close. People always leave.*

The enemy loves to reinforce that fear with every disappointment. But God's Word gently cuts through that lie.

David wrote, *"Though my father and mother forsake me, the Lord will receive me."* He knew what it felt like to be overlooked, misunderstood, and betrayed. Yet, he anchored his identity not in who walked away, but in the One who stayed. God's presence is not based on convenience. It's covenant. And His loyalty never changes.

Even when others walk out, **God remains fully present.** And not only that, He promises to bring people into your life who are led by His love. People who won't just be around when it's easy, but who will stand by you when it's hard.

You are not destined to be alone. You are surrounded by a love that stays *and He will send those who are meant to walk with you.*

PRAYER:

Lord, heal the wounds of abandonment that weigh on my heart. Remind me that Your presence is constant and unshakeable. Surround me with people who reflect Your faithfulness and help me trust in Your unfailing love. Amen.

AFFIRMATION:

Even if people leave, God remains. And He's bringing loyal, godly relationships.

Lie #19

IF YOU SET BOUNDARIES, THEY'LL STOP LOVING YOU

Truth: *"Love does not dishonor others… it is not self-seeking… it always protects."*
(1 Corinthians 13:5–7) **NIV**

REFLECTION:

For many, setting boundaries feels like a risk, a risk of being misunderstood, rejected, or even unloved.

Maybe you've been the one who says yes when you really want to say no. The friend who always shows up, even when you're running on empty. The parent who never takes a break out of fear that their rest will be mistaken for neglect. Slowly, the fear takes root: *If I protect my peace, I might lose people. If I draw a line, I might lose love.*

But that's a lie, and Jesus Himself proves it.

Jesus, the embodiment of perfect love, practiced boundaries often. He stepped away from crowds to rest. He removed Himself from toxic conversations. He said no to demands that didn't align with the Father's will. And in doing so, He showed us that **boundaries are not selfish, they are sacred.**

Healthy boundaries do not push away real love. They **protect it.** They guard your mental, emotional, and spiritual well-being so you can love from a place of wholeness instead of exhaustion.

If someone walks away because you established a boundary, they were not rooted in love, they were attached to your availability, not your value. *Boundaries protect your peace, and real love will honor them.*

PRAYER:

Father, grant me the courage to set boundaries without fear. Teach me that true love respects limits and reflects Your heart of protection. Surround me with relationships that thrive on respect, not control. Amen.

AFFIRMATION:

Boundaries are sacred. I safeguard my peace, and God honors that.

_____

_____

_____

_____

_____

_____

_____

_____

_____

Lie #20

YOU HAVE TO SETTLE TO BE LOVED

Truth: *"No good thing does he withhold from those whose walk is blameless."* (Psalm 84:11) **ESV**

REFLECTION:

Desperation can distort discernment.

It convinces you that loneliness is worse than compromise. That half-love is better than no love. That if you don't lower your standards, you'll miss your only shot at being chosen. Slowly, the enemy twists your waiting into panic and whispers the lie: *If you don't settle, you'll end up alone.*

But the truth is this, **settling for less than God's best is never the answer. You were made for more than crumbs.**

Ruth had every reason to choose survival over purpose. After loss and grief, she could have returned to familiarity and convenience. But instead, she stayed loyal to Naomi and faithful to God. That faithfulness positioned her to meet Boaz, a man of integrity, honor, and covenant love. Their story wasn't rushed. It was orchestrated. And it reminds us that **waiting well leads to receiving well.**

God is not holding out on you. He is holding **something up**, preparing what is good, whole, and aligned with your value. You were never meant to settle for relationships that drain you, ignore your worth, or force you to shrink.

You are worth love that is healthy, holy, and honest.

PRAYER:

Lord, protect my heart from the fear that pushes me to settle. Help me trust Your timing and believe that what You have prepared for me is good. Teach me to walk uprightly and wait with faith. Amen.

AFFIRMATION:

I refuse to settle. God's best for me is worth the wait.

_____

_____

_____

_____

_____

_____

_____

_____

_____

_____

_____

Lie #21

GOD IS DISAPPOINTED IN YOU

Truth: *"Therefore, there is now no condemnation for those who are in Christ Jesus."* (Romans 8:1) **NLT**

REFLECTION:

This lie often speaks the loudest right after a fall.

You said you'd never go back to that habit but you did. You promised to pray more, read more, trust more but you didn't. And suddenly, the silence feels heavier. The guilt feels louder. The enemy begins to whisper: *God is shaking His head at you. You've let Him down again.*

But that's not the heart of your Father.

Peter denied Jesus three times. Not privately, but publicly. And not once, but repeatedly. If anyone had reason to believe they had disappointed God beyond recovery, it was Peter. Yet after the resurrection, Jesus didn't come to scold him. He came to **restore him**.

On the shore of Galilee, Jesus asked Peter three times, *"Do you love Me?"* Not to shame him, but to reaffirm his calling. Peter didn't find judgment that morning. He found mercy, grace, and a fresh start.

God is not waiting for you to get it all right. He's waiting for you to come close again. His love doesn't break when you fall. It reaches in and lifts you back up. *God is still working in you, and His mercy is stronger than your mistakes.*

PRAYER:

Father, thank You for Your unwavering grace. Heal the wounds of shame that suggest You are disappointed in me. Help me walk confidently in Your love and live free from condemnation. Amen.

AFFIRMATION:

God delights in me. His grace covers me, and His love never abandons me.

Lie #22

GOD'S NOT LISTENING

Truth: *"The Lord hears his people when they call to him for help. He rescues them from all their troubles."* (Psalm 34:17) **NLT**

REFLECTION:

There's something about silence that can feel like rejection.

You pour your heart out. You fast. You cry. You beg God to move, but nothing seems to change. Days turn into weeks. Months stretch into years. And in that space, the enemy slips in and whispers: *God's ignoring you. Your prayers don't matter. He's not listening.*

But silence is not the same as absence.

Hannah knew this struggle well. She prayed for years with no answer, longing for a child while being mocked by those around her. Heaven felt quiet, but she kept praying. And when the time was right, God moved. Her son Samuel didn't just bring joy to her household, he became a prophet who shaped Israel's future. **God wasn't ignoring her. He was aligning her request with divine timing.**

Sometimes God's answer is "wait." Sometimes it's "not yet." But it is **never** "I don't care."

Your cries are not forgotten. Your tears are not wasted. Scripture promises that God collects every tear and hears every whisper. Even when you don't feel Him, **He is listening, and He is working.**

PRAYER:

Lord, thank You for hearing even the quietest cries of my heart. Strengthen me when the silence feels heavy, and remind me that You are always listening and working for my good. Amen.

AFFIRMATION:

God hears me. My prayers matter, and He's working behind the scenes.

Lie #23

GOD'S PROMISES AREN'T FOR YOU

Truth: *"For no matter how many promises God has made, they are 'Yes' in Christ. And so through him the 'Amen' is spoken by us to the glory of God."*
(2 Corinthians 1:20) **NIV**

REFLECTION:

It's hard to hold onto a promise when your life looks nothing like it.

You see others walk into healing, breakthrough, and open doors, while you're still praying, still waiting, still wondering. You read verses about God's goodness, His provision, His peace, but your circumstances feel like the opposite. That's when the enemy starts whispering: *God meant that for someone else, not for you. You must have been skipped.*

But God does not write promises He doesn't plan to keep.

Abraham's story is a testimony to that truth. God told him he would be the father of nations, but year after year, the promise seemed more distant. He and Sarah grew old, and the waiting grew long. But God had not forgotten. At the appointed time, Isaac was born, not a minute early, not a second late. **God fulfilled what He promised, just as He said.**

You are not excluded from the covenant. You are not invisible to heaven. God's promises are not performance-based, they are **grace-based**, sealed in the finished work of Jesus.

If He spoke it, He will perform it. And just because it hasn't happened yet doesn't mean it never will. *Every promise in Christ is a 'yes' and you are included in that yes.*

PRAYER:

Father, thank You for the certainty of Your promises, which are sealed in Christ. Help me reject the lie of exclusion and embrace every word You have spoken. Teach me to wait in faith, knowing You are faithful to fulfill Your promises. Amen.

AFFIRMATION:

God's promises are for me, and I respond "yes" to them by faith.

Lie #24

GOD DOESN'T CARE ABOUT THE SMALL STUFF

Truth: *"Indeed, the very hairs of your head are all numbered. Don't be afraid; you are worth more than many sparrows."* (Luke 12:7) **NIV**

REFLECTION:

This lie whispers in moments of quiet hesitation.

You're about to pray about something that feels small, a deadline, a decision, a financial need, an emotional weight, and suddenly you wonder: *Does God really care about this? Isn't He too busy handling bigger things?* The enemy leans in and says, *This isn't spiritual enough. God doesn't bother with this kind of stuff.*

But Jesus proved otherwise.

At a wedding in Cana, the wine ran out. It wasn't a crisis of life and death. It wasn't a national emergency. But it mattered to the hosts. And because it mattered to them, it mattered to Jesus. He didn't roll His eyes or rebuke their request, He responded. With a miracle. **Water into wine. Disappointment into joy. Small detail into divine display.**

That moment shows us something profound: **God is not just the Lord of the big picture. He's also the God of the tiny details.**

If He numbers the hairs on your head, He sees the weight you carry. The group chat that stressed you out. The class you're nervous about. The rent you're unsure how to pay. The unspoken fear that feels silly but still sits heavy. None of it is beneath Him.

You don't need to filter your prayers. You just need to bring them. *If it matters to you, it matters to God.*

PRAYER:

Lord, thank You for caring about the details of my life. Teach me to confidently bring every concern, large or small, before You. Remind me daily that nothing about me is beneath Your attention. Amen.

AFFIRMATION:

God is in the details. Nothing in my life is beneath His care.

Lie #25

YOU'VE GONE TOO FAR FOR GOD TO STILL LOVE YOU

Truth: *"But where sin increased, grace increased all the more."* (Romans 5:20) **NIV**

REFLECTION:

Guilt has a way of making the distance between you and God feel unbridgeable.

Maybe it's been years since you prayed. Maybe you've made choices you swore you'd never make. Maybe you've asked for forgiveness before, only to fall again, and now shame whispers, *That was the last straw. You've gone too far. God is done with you.*

But here's the truth: **God doesn't draw lines to keep you out, He builds bridges to bring you home.**

The prodigal son knew failure intimately. He took his father's inheritance and squandered it in rebellion. He ended up in a place of complete desperation, assuming that returning home meant punishment. But the moment he came into view, his father ran to him. No delay. No lecture. Just open arms, a fresh robe, and the words that matter most: *"This is my son."*

This story isn't just about a wayward son. **It's a picture of God's heart for every one of us.**

There is no sin too dark, no distance too great, and no past too heavy that can overpower the love of God. The cross already settled it. Jesus didn't die for the cleaned-up version of you, He died for the real you, mess and all.

You don't have to fix yourself before coming back. You just have to come.

God's love has no limit, and He's waiting with arms wide open.

PRAYER:

Lord, thank You that no sin is stronger than Your grace. Break the chains of shame and remind me that Your arms are always open. Help me believe that I am never too far gone for Your love. Amen.

AFFIRMATION:

God's grace is greater than my past. I can always come home to Him.

_____

_____

_____

_____

_____

_____

_____

Lie #26
IT'S TOO LATE TO START OVER

Truth: *"See, I am doing a new thing! Now it springs up; do you not perceive it? I am making a way in the wilderness and streams in the wasteland."* (Isaiah 43:19) **NIV**

REFLECTION:

This lie usually shows up when we start counting time instead of trusting God.

You look back and see missed opportunities, failed relationships, or dreams you buried under years of disappointment. Maybe you think you're too old, too late, or too far behind. The enemy leans in and whispers: *That window closed. That season is over. Starting fresh isn't for you anymore.*

But that's not what God says.

Abraham and Sarah had every natural reason to believe their time had passed. Their bodies said no. Their age said no. Even their faith wavered at times. Yet God had the final word, and that word was *"Yes."* In their old age, they received a miracle child named Isaac. Their story is living proof that **God is not confined by clocks or calendars.**

With God, **you don't age out of purpose.** You don't time out of grace. He can breathe life into what you thought was dead and restore what you thought was wasted.

You haven't missed your moment, you're standing on the edge of a new one. We serve a God *who makes all things new, and it's not too late for you.*

PRAYER:

Lord, thank You for being the God of fresh starts. Heal the regret of wasted years and restore hope for what lies ahead. Teach me to believe that You are making all things new. Amen.

AFFIRMATION:

God makes all things new, including me. I'm never too late for His plan.

Lie #27

THINGS WILL NEVER GET BETTER

Truth: *"Weeping may stay for the night, but rejoicing comes in the morning."* (Psalm 30:5) **NIV**

REFLECTION:

When life feels like one long night, it's easy to assume the sun won't rise again.

Financial hardship. Chronic illness. Deep grief. Lingering disappointment. These aren't just situations, they're seasons. And when the season feels never-ending, the enemy seizes the moment, whispering: *This is your new normal. Get used to the pain. Hope is for other people.*

But that's not the voice of truth.

Job's story reminds us that pain doesn't have the final word. He lost nearly everything: his children, his health, his wealth, and even his sense of purpose. His friends misunderstood him. His wife told him to give up. And yet, **God was not done.** The same God who allowed the testing ultimately brought the restoring.

Job's end was greater than his beginning. His weeping didn't last forever. And neither will yours.

Yes, there are seasons that stretch us. But they are just that, **seasons**, not life sentences. God specializes in turning mourning into dancing, ashes into beauty, and despair into destiny.

God's not finished with you. Your greater days are still ahead. You're not stuck, you're being strengthened. Keep walking. The valley is not your home. God's not just going to bring you out. He's going to bring you out better.

PRAYER:

Lord, thank You that sorrow is not the end of my story. Strengthen me during the night seasons and remind me that joy is coming. Fill my heart with hope that You are still working, even when life feels heavy. Amen.

AFFIRMATION:

This isn't the end of my story. Morning is coming, and joy is on the way.

_____

_____

_____

_____

_____

_____

_____

_____

_____

Lie #28

THIS STRUGGLE IS FOREVER

Truth: *"No temptation has overtaken you except what is common to mankind. And God is faithful; he will not let you be tempted beyond what you can bear. But when you are tempted, he will also provide a way out so that you can endure it."* (1 Corinthians 10:13) **NIV**

REFLECTION:

When a struggle lingers, it can start to feel like a life sentence.

The person who's relapsed again starts to wonder if freedom is even possible. The woman battling anxiety wakes up exhausted, wondering if peace is just a word people use in church. The family stuck in cycles of tension may begin to accept dysfunction as the norm. And right in the middle of it all, the enemy leans in and whispers: *This is your forever.*

But that's a lie wrapped in fatigue. And God has something better to say.

Consider Israel. For over 400 years, generation after generation lived under the whip of Egyptian slavery. Children were born into bondage. Hope was passed down like a bedtime story, but freedom seemed out of reach. Still, God never forgot. At just the right time, He raised up Moses, shook Egypt to its knees, parted the sea, and ushered His people out, not limping, but **liberated**.

The same God who ended generations of slavery can bring an end to your struggle. Your cycle isn't stronger than His covenant. Your weakness isn't greater than His power. Your fight isn't forever, even if it's been long, it won't be **endless**.

The enemy wants you exhausted, discouraged, and resigned. But God is strengthening you, sustaining you, and planning your way out. This struggle has an expiration date, and your breakthrough is already on heaven's calendar.

PRAYER:

Lord, thank You that no battle lasts forever. Remind me that You are faithful to provide strength and a way through. Help me view my struggles as temporary seasons, not permanent identities. Amen.

AFFIRMATION:

This battle won't break me. I'm not stuck; I'm coming through stronger.

_____

_____

_____

_____

_____

_____

_____

Lie #29

YOUR BEST DAYS ARE BEHIND YOU

Truth: *"The glory of this present house will be greater than the glory of the former house,' says the Lord Almighty."* (Haggai 2:9) **NIV**

REFLECTION:

This lie often sneaks in during moments of reflection when you're scrolling through old photos, remembering seasons when life felt more vibrant, purposeful, or exciting.

It sounds like: *"You peaked back then. Now, you're just coasting."*

An older adult may feel like their influence has faded. A dreamer who once dared to hope may now quietly settle for survival. A person who walked through divorce, disappointment, or job loss might believe joy like that will never return.

And right then, the enemy whispers: *"Those were the good days. You missed your moment."*

But Scripture paints a different picture.

Caleb was 85, and still believed for more. After decades of delay in the wilderness, he didn't retire, he *re-fired*. He stood before Joshua and boldly said, *"Give me this mountain… I'm just as strong now as I was then."* Caleb's faith teaches us that God doesn't count you out when the calendar moves forward. If anything, He's just getting started.

You're not too old.

You're not too late.

And you're not too far from new victories.

The enemy will make nostalgia look like your peak. But God doesn't do reruns, He does new, better, and beyond. Your story isn't winding down, it's leveling up. Every chapter with God leads upward.

If you're still breathing, God's still building. Your best days are not behind you. They're just ahead.

PRAYER:

Lord, thank You that with You, the future is always bright. Break the grip of nostalgia that makes me believe the best is behind me. Fill my heart with hope that greater glory lies ahead. Amen.

AFFIRMATION:

My future is bright. God is continuously working greater things in me and through me.

Lie #30

YOU'LL ALWAYS BE STUCK

Truth: *"So if the Son sets you free, you will be free indeed."* (John 8:36) **NIV**

REFLECTION:

This lie is suffocating. It wraps around your mind in moments of frustration, failure, or delay. It tells you: *"This is just how life is now. You'll never change. You'll never move forward."*

It whispers to the one battling a private addiction. It torments the one drowning in financial pressure. It discourages the dreamer who keeps hitting closed doors.

And then the enemy seals it with this deceptive final blow: *"You'll never be free. You'll always be stuck."*

But Scripture breaks that narrative.

Paul and Silas were locked in a prison: physically bound, unfairly treated, and seemingly forgotten. Yet in the middle of the night, they didn't give in to despair. They *sang*. They *worshiped*. And suddenly, the prison shook. Chains fell. Doors opened. Freedom came.

Not because they forced their way out, but because they *invited God in*.

Your prison isn't permanent. Your cycle isn't your sentence. And delay doesn't mean denial.

The enemy wants you to believe you'll always be in this cycle of: sin, sadness, shame, or stagnation. Jesus didn't just save you, He freed you. Stuck is not your story's ending.

Every negative season and cycle has an expiration date with God. You may feel delayed, but you're not defeated. Freedom is already yours.

PRAYER:

Lord, thank You for breaking every chain that holds me captive. Remind me that freedom is my inheritance in Christ. Help me step boldly into the future You have prepared, no longer stuck but fully alive in You. Amen.

AFFIRMATION:

I am free in Christ. I am not stuck; I am stepping into freedom, one step at a time.

CONCLUSION: AFTER 30 DAYS, WHAT NEXT?

You've just completed 30 days of uncovering lies and embracing God's truth. That's a significant accomplishment. It takes bravery to face the enemy's whispers and humility to let God's Word reshape your view of yourself, your relationships, and your future.

But this isn't the end, it's just the beginning. Freedom in Christ isn't a one-time event; it's a daily choice. Just as lies can quietly creep back in, you must intentionally guard and rehearse the truth. What you've started in these 30 days is a fresh rhythm: listening for God's voice above all others, anchoring your identity in Christ, and living out the promises of His Word.

So, what comes next?

- **Keep feeding on truth.** Don't close your Bible now that these 30 days are over.

Continue exploring the Scriptures for God's promises and speak them over your life. Truth is the only weapon strong enough to silence lies.

- **Keep renewing your mind.** Transformation occurs as your thoughts are reshaped day by day. Make it a habit to ask yourself: *What lie is trying to speak here? What truth from God's Word replaces it?*

- **Keep walking in community.** Lies lose their power in the light. Share your journey with others. Surround yourself with people who will remind you of who you are in Christ when you forget.

- **Keep declaring victory.** Lies may try to return, but you don't have to let them in. Keep affirming God's Word over your life. Keep praying. Keep standing.

These thirty days may have brought you freedom in some areas and opened your eyes in others, but God is still at work. His Spirit continues the process of renewal, healing, and transformation far beyond these pages.

So step forward with confidence. This is not the end of your journey. It marks the beginning of a life lived in the light of God's truth; free, whole, and unshakable in Christ.

When you know the truth, you can never believe the lie again.

www.ingramcontent.com/pod-product-compliance
Lightning Source LLC
LaVergne TN
LVHW051848080426
835512LV00018B/3134